Facts About the Amur Leopard

By Lisa Strattin

© 2016 Lisa Strattin

Revised 2022 © Lisa Strattin

FREE BOOK

FREE FOR ALL SUBSCRIBERS

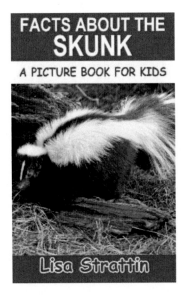

LisaStrattin.com/Subscribe-Here

BOX SET

- **FACTS ABOUT THE POISON DART FROGS**
- **FACTS ABOUT THE THREE TOED SLOTH**
- **FACTS ABOUT THE RED PANDA**
- **FACTS ABOUT THE SEAHORSE**
- **FACTS ABOUT THE PLATYPUS**
- **FACTS ABOUT THE REINDEER**
- **FACTS ABOUT THE PANTHER**
- **FACTS ABOUT THE SIBERIAN HUSKY**

LisaStrattin.com/BookBundle

Facts for Kids Picture Books by Lisa Strattin

Little Blue Penguin, Vol 92

Chipmunk, Vol 5

Frilled Lizard, Vol 39

Blue and Gold Macaw, Vol 13

Poison Dart Frogs, Vol 50

Blue Tarantula, Vol 115

African Elephants, Vol 8

Amur Leopard, Vol 89

Sabre Tooth Tiger, Vol 167

Baboon, Vol 174

Sign Up for New Release Emails Here

LisaStrattin.com/subscribe-here

★★COVER IMAGE★★

https://www.flickr.com/photos/zoofanatic/30242174876/

★★ADDITIONAL IMAGES★★

https://www.flickr.com/photos/macjewell/3178155138/

https://www.flickr.com/photos/elpadawan/7197131214/

https://www.flickr.com/photos/tasshu113/4956301449/

https://www.flickr.com/photos/96541566@N06/51714288289/

https://www.flickr.com/photos/smerikal/7900697258/

https://www.flickr.com/photos/hisgett/5017704631/

https://www.flickr.com/photos/hisgett/48240936321/

https://www.flickr.com/photos/zoofanatic/36534200803/

https://www.flickr.com/photos/jim_wilson_photos/50281472293/

https://www.flickr.com/photos/zoofanatic/28004147795/

Contents

INTRODUCTION

The Amur Leopard is a subspecies of leopard that lives in the temperate forests of eastern Russia and northern China. It is also known as the *Far East Leopard*, *Manchurian Leopard*, and *Korean Leopard*. The scientific name of the Amur Leopard is *Panthera Pardis Orientalis*. It is the rarest big cat in the world and is critically endangered.

Amur Leopards, while not as large as some of the other big cats, are very powerful. They are fast, and can run, leap, jump high in the air, climb, and swim. They use their strength and speed to protect themselves from human hunting and to attack large prey. Amur Leopards hunt for prey alone and spend most of their lives alone. Their fur acts as camouflage and helps to conceal them in the dense forest. It also grows thick and dense to keep them warm during the cold winter.

CHARACTERISTICS

Amur Leopards are large, strong, powerful animals. They are also very fast. They can run at a speed of up to 37 miles per hour! Amur Leopards are very good jumpers as well. They can leap as far as 19 feet horizontally and as high as 10 feet vertically. Amur Leopards can also climb and swim well.

They have large heads with strong neck and jaw muscles. They use these strong muscles, along with their excellent vision, to hunt hoofed mammals. They can attack and kill prey up to 10 times their own weight. Their good eyesight and hearing help them to find prey in the dense forests where they live. They do most of their hunting in the early morning and evening. In the middle of the day, they rest.

Amur Leopards are solitary. They live and hunt alone. Females with young are the only exception. The females will hunt with their offspring until the young ones can care for themselves. They are territorial, and live and hunt in an area that is normally about 30 square miles in size. The territory of one Amur Leopard may overlap slightly with the territory of another.

APPEARANCE

Amur Leopards have fur that helps them to maintain their ideal body temperature. It also serves to camouflage them in their habitat. The fur can be shades of yellow, golden, and red, with dark spots. In the summer, the fur is darker and shows more vivid coloring. In the winter, the color of their fur becomes lighter. This helps to conceal them in the snowy winter environment. Amur Leopard fur also grows longer and thicker as the weather gets colder. In summer, the fur is about an inch long. In winter, it can grow up to 2 ¾ inches. These animals have long legs, which help them walk in deep snow.

LIFE STAGES

The female gives birth to 1 to 4 cubs at one time, with each cub weighing less than two pounds. The birthing season is normally in late spring or early summer. The babies' eyes are closed for the first week and they are totally helpless and depend on their mother's care. The mother keeps them hidden while she hunts. She moves them often to protect them from predators.

At about 2 weeks old, the babies can walk. They are weaned at around 3 months. The mother teaches her babies how to hunt, and the young remain with her for 18 to 24 months.

LIFE SPAN

Amur Leopards live 10 to 15 years in the wild, and up to 20 years in captivity.

SIZE

Male Amur Leopards are larger than the females. The males weigh between 80 and 200 pounds, while the females weigh 60 to 135 pounds.

HABITAT

Amur Leopards live in temperate forests in eastern Russia and northern China. The climate can be warm in the summer and is very cold in the winter, so their fur grows longer and thicker to respond to the cooling temperature.

DIET

Amur Leopards are carnivores. They hunt Roe Deer, Sitka Deer, and Musk Deer. They hide their killed prey in trees and come back to eat it later. Sometimes they store several kills at once. Occasionally, they may kill smaller animals such as rabbits or owls.

ENEMIES

For a variety of reasons, people are the primary enemy of the Amur Leopard. Humans hunt them for their fur and bones. The bones are used in some traditional Asian medicines. Humans also hunt them to protect livestock, which Amur Leopards sometimes attack and kill. Because of hunting by humans, the Amur Leopard is classified as critically endangered. As of this writing, there are thought to be only 50 to 60 animals remaining in their natural habitat.

SUITABILITY AS PETS

Amur Leopards are dangerous wild animals and should never be kept as pets. They are solitary, not comfortable around humans, and could do serious damage with their strong jaws and teeth.

COLOR ME

COLOR ME

COLOR ME

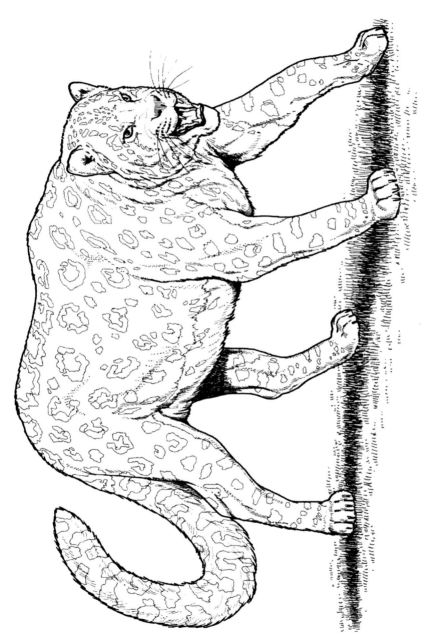

COLOR ME

COLOR ME

COLOR ME

COLOR ME

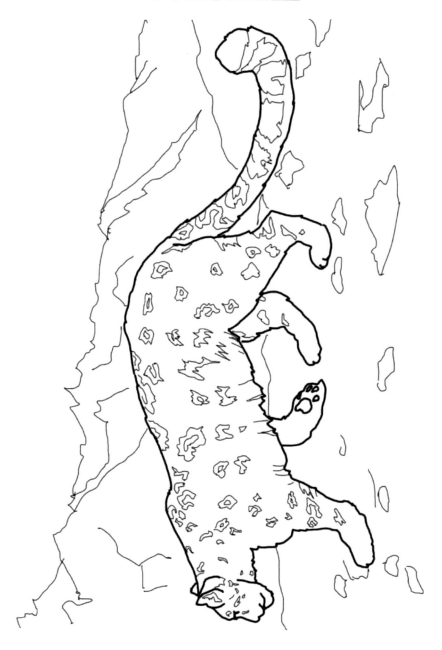

COLOR ME

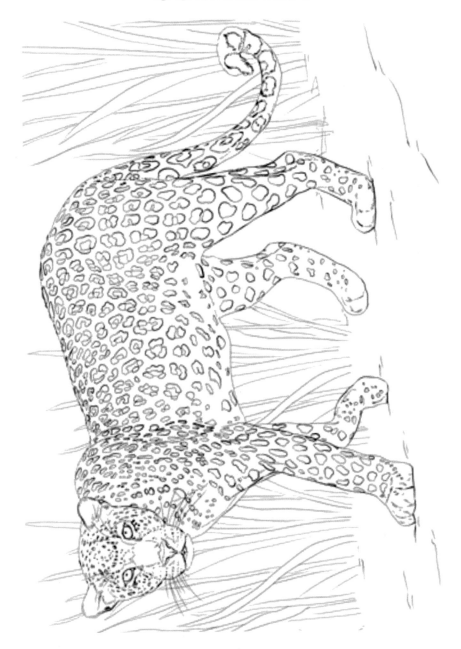

COLOR ME

COLOR ME

Please leave me a review here:

LisaStrattin.com/Review-Vol-89

For more Kindle Downloads Visit Lisa Strattin Author Page on Amazon Author Central

amazon.com/author/lisastrattin

To see upcoming titles, visit my website at LisaStrattin.com– most books available on Kindle!

LisaStrattin.com

FREE BOOK

FOR ALL SUBSCRIBERS – SIGN UP NOW

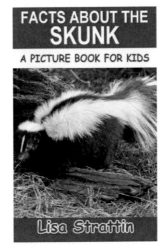

LisaStrattin.com/Subscribe-Here

LisaStrattin.com/Facebook

LisaStrattin.com/Youtube

Made in the USA
Monee, IL
14 March 2023

29900527R00026